Little Book

DEVOTIONS

31 DAILY DEVOTIONALS

Kindness

Little Book

DEVOTIONS

Kindness

ISBN 1-58334-190-0

The quoted ideas expressed in this book (but not scripture verses) are not, in all cases, exact quotations, as some have been edited for clarity and brevity. In all cases, the author has attempted to maintain the speaker's original intent. In some cases, quoted material for this book was obtained from secondary sources, primarily print media. While every effort was made to ensure the accuracy of these sources, the accuracy cannot be guaranteed. For additions, deletions, corrections or clarifications in future editions of this text, please write BIRGHTON BOOKS.

Scripture taken from the HOLY BIBLE, NEW INTERNATIONAL VERSION ©. NIV ©. Copyright © 1973, 1978, 1984, by International Bible Society. Used by permission of Zondervan Publishing House. All rights reserved.

Scripture quoted from the *International Children's Bible®, New Century Version®*, copyright © 1986,1988,1999 by Tommy Nelson™, a division of Thomas Nelson, Inc. Nashville, Tennessee 37214. Used by permission.

Scripture quotations marked (TLB) are taken from The Holy Bible, The Living Bible Translation, Copyright © 1971. Used by permission of Tyndale House Publishers, Incorporated, Wheaton, Illinois 60189. All rights reserved.

Scripture quotations marked (NLT) are taken from The Holy Bible, New Living Translation, Copyright © 1996. Used by permission of Tyndale House Publishers, Incorporated, Wheaton, Illinois 60189. All rights reserved.

Scripture taken from the NEW AMERICAN STANDARD BIBLE®, Copyright © 1960, 1962, 1963, 1968, 1971, 1972, 1973, 1975, 1977, 1995 by The Lockman Foundation. Used by permission.

Printed in the United States of America
Cover Design: Kim Russel, Wahoo Designs
Page Layout: Bart Dawson

1 2 3 4 5 6 7 8 9 10 • 02 03 04 05 06 07 08 09 10

For All of God's Children

Table of Contents

A Message
to Parents

Perhaps your child's library is already overflowing with brightly colored children's books. If so, congratulations: you're a thoughtful parent who understands the importance of reading to young children.

This little book is an important addition to your child's library. It is intended to be read *by* Christian parents *to* their young children. The text contains 31 brief chapters, one for each day of the month. Each chapter contains a Bible verse, a brief story or lesson, tips for kids and parents, and a prayer. The chapters examine a different aspect of an important Biblical theme: kindness.

For the next 31 days, try this experiment: read one chapter each night to your child, and then spend a few more moments talking about the chapter's meaning. By the end of the month, you will have had 31 different opportunities to share God's wisdom with your son or daughter, and that's a very good thing.

If you have been touched by God's love and His grace, then you know the joy that He has brought into your own life. Now it's your turn to share His message with the boy or girl whom He has entrusted to your care. Happy reading! And may God richly bless you and your family now and forever.

Kindness

The Golden Rule

Do for other people the same things you
want them to do for you.

☆☆☆

Matthew 7:12 ICB

Some rules are easier to understand than they are to live by. Jesus told us that we should treat other people in the same way that we would want to be treated: that's the Golden Rule. But sometimes, especially when we're tired or upset, that rule is very hard to follow.

Jesus wants us to treat other people with respect, love, kindness, and courtesy. When we do, we make our families and friends happy . . . and we make our Father in heaven very proud. So if you're wondering how to treat someone else, ask the person you see every time you look into the mirror. The answer you receive will tell you exactly what to do.

KID TIP

What's good for you is good for them, too: If you want others to treat *you* according to the Golden Rule, then you should be quick to treat them in the same way. In other words, always play by the rule: the Golden Rule.

WOW

It's not difficult to make the world a better place. All you really have to do is put the needs of others ahead of your own. You can make a difference with a little time and a big heart.

James Dobson

Parent Tip

Make sure that *your* Rule is Golden, too: Kids imitate parents, so act accordingly! The best way for your child to learn the Golden Rule is by example . . . *your* example!

19

Dear Lord,
let me treat others as I want
to be treated. Let me be kind,
let me wait my turn, let me
share, and let me treat
everyone fairly. I want to keep
the Golden Rule today and
every day, Lord, so that I
will be the kind of person that
Jesus wants me to be.

Amen

2

Be Kind to Everyone

Show respect for all people.
Love the brothers and sisters
of God's family.

✰✰✰

1 Peter 2:17 ICB

Who deserves our respect? Grown-ups? Of course. Teachers? Certainly. Family members? Yes. Friends? That's right, but it doesn't stop there. The Bible teaches us to treat *all* people with respect.

Respect for others is habit-forming: the more we do it, the easier it becomes. So start practicing right now. Say lots of kind words and do lots of kind things, because when it comes to kindness and respect, practice makes perfect.

Respecting all kinds of people: Make sure that you show proper respect for everyone, even if that person happens to be different from you. It's easy to make fun of people who seem different . . . but it's wrong.

WOW
We can always gauge our actions by the teachings of Jesus Christ.

Oswald Chambers

It starts with you: Remember: Kindness, dignity, and respect for others begins at the head of the household and works its way down from there. And our kids are *always* watching!

Dear Lord,
help me to be kind to
everyone I meet. Help me to
be respectful to all people, not
just teachers and parents. Help
me to say kind words and do good
deeds, today and every day.

Amen

Doing the Right Thing

Doing what is right brings freedom
to honest people.

☆☆☆

Proverbs 11:6 ICB

Sometimes, it's so much easier to do the wrong thing than it is to do the right thing, especially when we're tired or frustrated. But, doing the wrong thing almost always leads to trouble. And sometimes, it leads to BIG trouble.

When you do the right thing, you don't have to worry about what you did or what you said. But, when you do the wrong thing, you'll be worried that someone will find out. So do the right thing; it may be harder in the beginning, but it's easier in the end.

Think ahead: Before you do something, ask yourself this question: "Will I be ashamed if my parents find out?" If the answer to that question is "Yes," don't do it!

WOW

But now you are children of God
who obey. Be holy in all that you do,
just as God is holy.

1 Peter 1:14-15 ICB

See as much as you can; correct as much as you should: Encouraging children to do the right thing requires an observing eye and a patient heart. Expect your children to be well-behaved, but don't expect them to be perfect. In fact, an important part of parenting is knowing *what* to overlook and *when* to overlook it.

Dear Lord,
I want to be a person who
respects others, and I want
to be a person who is kind.
Wherever I am and whatever I
do, let me be like Jesus in the
way that I treat others, because
with Him as my guide, I will do
the right thing, today and
forever.

Amen

Saying 4 Nice Things

When you talk, do not say harmful things.
But say what people need—words that will
help them become stronger. Then what you
say will help those who listen to you.

☆☆☆

Ephesians 4:29 ICB

Do you like for people to say kind words to you? Of course you do! And that's exactly how other people feel, too. That's why it's so important to say things that make people feel better, not worse.

Your words can help people . . . or not. Make certain that you're the kind of person who says helpful things, not hurtful things. And, make sure that you're the kind of person who helps other people feel better about themselves, not worse.

Everybody needs to hear kind words, and that's exactly the kind of words they should hear *from you!*

KiD TiP

If you can't think of something nice to say . . . don't say anything. It's better to say nothing than to hurt someone's feelings.

WOW

Make it a rule, and pray to God to help you to keep it, never to lie down at night without being able to say: "I have made at least one human being a little wiser, a little happier, or a little better this day.

Charles Kingsley

Parent Tip

And seldom is heard a discouraging word: If it's good enough for "Home on the Range," it's good enough for your home, too. Make certain that your little abode is a haven of encouragement for every member of your family. You do so by checking your gripes and disappointments at the front door . . . and encouraging everybody else to do like-wise!

31

PRAY TIME

Dear Lord,
I want my words to help
other people. Let me choose
my words and my actions
carefully so that when I speak,
the world is a better place
because of the things I have
said and the things I have done.

Amen

5

God Knows
the Heart

I am the Lord, and I can look
into a person's heart.

☆☆☆

Jeremiah 17:10 ICB

You can try to keep secrets from other people, but you can't keep secrets from God. God knows what you think and what you do. And, if you want to please God, you must start with good intentions and a pure heart.

If your heart tells you not to do something, don't do it! If your conscience tells you that something is wrong, stop! If you feel ashamed by something you've done, don't do it ever again! You can keep secrets from other people *some of the time*, but God is watching *all of the time*, and He sees everything, including your heart.

That little voice inside your head . . . is called your conscience. Listen to it; it's usually right!

WOW
To go against one's conscience
is neither safe nor right. Here I stand.
I cannot do otherwise.
Martin Luther

Teaching values: Your children will learn about life from many sources; the most important source can and should be you. But remember that the lectures you give are never as important as the ones you live.

Dear Lord,
other people see me from
the outside, but You know
my heart. Let my heart be pure,
and let me listen to the voice
that You have placed there,
today and always.

Amen

How Would Jesus Behave?

Love other people just as Christ loved us.

☆☆☆

Ephesians 5:2 ICB

If you're not sure whether something is right or wrong, ask yourself a simple question: "How would Jesus behave if He were here?" The answer to that question will tell you what to do.

Jesus was perfect, but we are not. Still, we must try *as hard* as we can to do *the best* that we can. When we do, we will love others, just as Christ loves us.

Kindness

KiD TiP

Learning about Jesus: Start learning about Jesus, and keep learning about Him as long as you live. His story never grows old, and His teachings never fail.

WOW

Tell me the story of Jesus.
Write on my heart every word.
Tell me the story most precious,
sweetest that ever was heard.

Fanny Crosby

Parent Tip

It's up to us: Our children will learn about Jesus at church and, in some cases, at school. But, the ultimate responsibility for religious teachings should never be delegated to institutions outside the home. As parents, *we* must teach our children about the love and grace of Jesus Christ by our words *and* by our actions.

Dear Lord,
let me use Jesus as my guide
for living. When I have questions
about what to do or how to act,
let me behave as He behaved.
When I do, I will share His love
with my family, with my friends,
and with the world.

Amen

Making 7 Friends

A friend loves you all the time.

☆☆☆

Proverbs 17:17 ICB

The Bible tells us that friendship can be a wonderful thing. That's why it's good to know how to make and to keep good friends.

If you want to make lots of friends, practice the Golden Rule with everybody you know. Be kind. Share. Say nice things. Be helpful. When you do, you'll discover that the Golden Rule isn't just a nice way to behave; it's also a great way to make and to keep friends!

First, become interested in them . . .and soon they'll become interested in you!

WOW
Friendship is one of
the sweetest joys of life.
C. H. Spurgeon

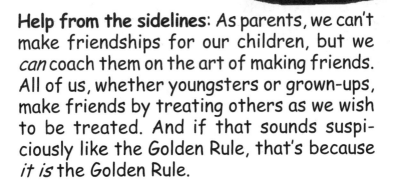

Help from the sidelines: As parents, we can't make friendships for our children, but we *can* coach them on the art of making friends. All of us, whether youngsters or grown-ups, make friends by treating others as we wish to be treated. And if that sounds suspiciously like the Golden Rule, that's because *it is* the Golden Rule.

Dear Lord,
help me to be a good friend.
Let me treat other people as
I want to be treated. Let me
share my things, and let me
share kind words with my friends
and family, today and every day.

Amen

8

God is Love

Whoever does not love does not know God,
because God is love.

☆☆☆

1 John 4:8 ICB

The Bible tells us that God is love and that if we wish to know Him, we must have love in our hearts. Sometimes, of course, when we're tired, frustrated, or angry, it is very hard for us to be loving. Thankfully, anger and frustration are feelings that come and go, but God's love lasts forever.

If you'd like to improve your day *and* your life, share God's love with your family and friends. Every time you love, and every time you give, God smiles.

Show and Tell: It's good to tell your loved ones how you feel about them, but that's not enough. You should also show them how you feel with your good deeds and your kind words.

WOW
He who is filled with love is filled with God Himself.

Saint Augustine

Be expressive: Make certain that at your house, love is expressed *and* demonstrated many times each day. Little acts of consideration and kindness can make a big difference in the way that your child views the world.

Dear Lord,
make me a person who is loving
and giving. You first loved me,
Father. Let me, in turn, love
others, and let my behavior
show them that I love them,
today and forever.

Amen

9

Paul and His Friends

I thank my God every time
I remember you.

☆☆☆

Philippians 1:3 NIV

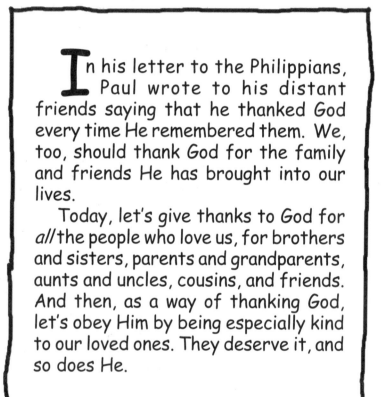

In his letter to the Philippians, Paul wrote to his distant friends saying that he thanked God every time He remembered them. We, too, should thank God for the family and friends He has brought into our lives.

Today, let's give thanks to God for *all* the people who love us, for brothers and sisters, parents and grandparents, aunts and uncles, cousins, and friends. And then, as a way of thanking God, let's obey Him by being especially kind to our loved ones. They deserve it, and so does He.

The mailman can help: If you have friends or relatives who are far away, send them letters or drawings (your mom or dad will be happy to mail them for you). Everybody loves to receive mail, and so will your family members and friends.

WOW
To love others is evidence of
our faith in God.
Kay Arthur

Help start the letter-writing habit early: Encourage your children to become world-class letter writers and top-flight "thank-you" note senders. Even in this age of electronic communication, nothing can take the place of an old-fashioned letter. And besides, without our children's notes and artwork, how would we decorate our refrigerators?

Dear Lord,
thank you for my family and my friends. Let me show kindness to *all* of them: those who are here at home *and* those who are far away. Then, my family and friends will know that I remember them and love them, today and every day.

Amen

10

Being Kind to Parents

Honor your father and your mother.

☆☆☆

Exodus 20:12 ICB

We love our parents *so* very much, but sometimes, we may take them for granted. When we take them "for granted," that means that we don't give them the honor and respect they deserve.

The Bible tells us to honor our parents. That's God's rule, and it's also the best way to live. When we treat our parents with the respect they deserve, we show them that we appreciate all they have done for us. And that's *so* much better than taking our parents for granted, and if you don't believe it, just ask them!

Two magic words: Thank you!: Your parents will never become tired of hearing those two little words. And while you're at it, try three more: "I love you!"

WOW
If we would think more,
we would thank more.
Warren Wiersbe

Old-fashioned respect never goes out of fashion: Remember the good old days when children were polite and respectful, especially to adults? For wise parents, those good old days are now.

Dear Lord,
make me respectful and thankful.
Let me give honor and love to my
parents, and let my behavior be
pleasing to them . . . and to You.

Amen

Happiness Is . . .

Those who want to do right more than
anything else are happy.

☆☆☆

Matthew 5:6 ICB

Do you want to be happy? Here are some things you should do: Love God and His Son, Jesus; obey the Golden Rule; and always try to do the right thing. When you do these things, you'll discover that happiness goes hand-in-hand with good behavior.

The happiest people do not misbehave; the happiest people are not cruel or greedy. The happiest people don't say unkind things. The happiest people are those who love God and follow his rules—starting, of course, with the Golden one.

Sometimes happy, sometimes not: Even if you're a *very* good person, you shouldn't expect to be happy *all* the time. Sometimes, things will happen to make you sad, and it's okay to be sad when bad things happen to you or to your friends and family. But remember: through good times and bad, you'll always be happier *if* you obey the rules of your Father in heaven. So obey them!

WOW

Happy is the person who . . .
loves what the Lord commands.

Psalm 112:1 ICB

In times of hardship: All families endure times of sadness or hardship; if your troubles seem overwhelming, be willing to seek outside help—starting, of course, with your pastor.

59

Dear Lord,
make me the kind of Christian
who earns happiness by doing the
right thing. When I obey your
rules, Father, I will find the joy
that you have in store for me.
Let me find Your joy, Lord, today
and always.

Amen

Solomon Says

12

A kind person is doing himself a favor.
But a cruel person brings trouble
upon himself.

☆☆☆

Proverbs 11:17 ICB

King Solomon wrote most of the Book of Proverbs; in it, he gave us wonderful advice for living wisely. Solomon warned that unkind behavior leads only to trouble, but kindness is its own reward.

The next time you're tempted to say an unkind word, remember Solomon. He was one of the wisest men who ever lived, and he knew that it's always better to be kind. And now, you know it, too.

Sorry you said it? Apologize! Did you say something that hurt someone's feelings? Then it's time for an apology: yours. It's never too late to apologize, but it's never too early, either!

WOW
Father, take our mistakes and
turn them into opportunities.

Max Lucado

Parents can apologize, too! Nobody's perfect, not even parents! If you say or do something you regret, apologize sooner rather than later. And, if that apology is owed to your spouse or to your child, be humble, be contrite, and be quick about it!

Dear Lord,
let me be a kind person. Let me
be quick to share and quick
to forgive. And when I make
mistakes, let me be quick to
change and quick to ask
forgiveness from others
and from You.

Amen

13
Love Your Enemies

I tell you, love your enemies.
Pray for those who hurt you.
If you do this, you will be true sons
of your Father in heaven.

☆☆☆

Matthew 6:44-45 ICB

It's easy to love people who have been nice to you, but it's very hard to love people who have treated you badly. Still, Jesus instructs us to treat both our friends *and* our enemies with kindness and respect.

Are you having problems being nice to someone? Is there someone you know whom you don't like very much? Remember that Jesus not only forgave His enemies, He also loved them . . . and so should you.

Making up may not be as hard as you think!
If there is someone who has been mean to
you, perhaps it's time for the two of you to
make up. If you're willing to be the first person to offer a kind word, you'll discover that
making up is usually easier than you think.

WOW

If you can't forgive others,
you break the bridge over which
you yourself must pass.

Corrie ten Boom

Holding a grudge? Drop it! How can you
expect your kids to forgive others if you
don't? Never expect your children to be
more forgiving than you are.

67

PRAY TIME

Dear Lord,
give me a forgiving heart.
When I have bad feelings toward
another person, help me to
forgive them and to love them,
just as You forgive and love me.

Amen

14

His Name Was Barnabas

Barnabas was a good man, full of the Holy Spirit and full of faith.

☆☆☆

Acts 11:23-24 ICB

Barnabas was a leader in the early Christian church who was known for his kindness and for his ability to encourage others. Because of Barnabas, many people were introduced to Christ.

We become like Barnabas when we speak kind words to our families and to our friends. And then, because we have been generous and kind, the people around us can see how Christians should behave. So when in doubt, be kind and generous to others, just like Barnabas.

Be an encourager! Barnabas was known as a man who encouraged others. In other words, he made other people feel better by saying kind things. You, like Barnabas, can encourage your family and friends . . . and you should.

WOW

A lot of people have gone further than they thought they could because someone else thought they could.

Zig Ziglar

Parents make the best encouragers! You're not just your children's parents; you're their biggest fans. Make sure they know it.

Dear Lord,
let me help to encourage other
people by the words that I say
and the things that I do. Let me
be a person who is always helpful
and kind to my friends and
family. And let them see Your
love for me reflected in
my love for them.

Amen

15

The Good Samaritan

Help each other with your troubles.
When you do this, you truly obey
the law of Christ.

☆☆☆

Galatians 6:2 ICB

Jesus told the story of a Jewish man who had been attacked by robbers. Luckily, a kind Samaritan happened by. And even though Jews and Samaritans were enemies, the Samaritan rescued the injured man.

And the meaning of the story is this: Jesus wants us to be kind to *everyone*, not just to our families and our friends. Jesus wants us to be good neighbors to *all people*, not just to those who are exactly like us.

Are you a good Samaritan? If so, you're doing the right thing, and that's exactly how God wants you to behave.

Amanda

KiD TiP

Look around: Someone very near you may need a helping hand or a kind word, so keep your eyes open, and look for people who need your help, whether at home, at church, or at school.

WOW

If we have the true love of God in our hearts, we will show it in our lives.

D. L. Moody

Parent Tip

Preach, teach, and reach . . . out!: When it comes to teaching our children about helping others, our sermons are not as important as our service. Charity should start at home—with parents—and work its way down the family tree from there.

75

PRAY TIME

Dear Lord,
make me a Good Samaritan.
Let me never be too busy or
too proud to help a person in
need. You have given me so many
blessings, Lord. Let me share
those blessings with others
today and every day that I live.

Amen

Tori

16

Don't Be Cruel!

Don't ever stop being kind and truthful.
Let kindness and truth show in all you do.

✩✩✩

Proverbs 3:3 ICB

Sometimes, young people can be very mean. They can make fun of other people, and when they do so, it's wrong. Period.

As Christians, we should be kind to everyone. And, if other kids say unkind things to a child or make fun of him or her, it's up to us to step in, like the Good Samaritan, and lend a helping hand.

Today and every day, be a person who is known for your kindness, not for your cruelty. That's how God wants you to behave. Period.

KiD TiP

Stand up and be counted! Do you know children who say or do cruel things to other kids? If so, don't join in! Instead, stand up for those who need your help. It's the right thing to do.

WOW
Preach the gospel at all times and,
if necessary, use words.

Saint Francis of Assisi

Parent Tip

When kids are mean: Face it: even the most angelic children can do things that are unfair or unkind. When we observe such behavior in our own children, we must be understanding, but firm. We live in a world where misbehavior is tolerated and, in many cases, glorified. But inside the walls of our own homes, misbehavior should never be ignored; it should be corrected by loving, courageous parents.

Dear Lord,
when I see meanness in this
world, let me do my best
to correct it. When I see people
who are hurting, let me do my
best to help them. And when I
am hurt by others, let me do my
best to forgive them.

Amen

17

When People Can't Help Themselves

I tell you the truth, whatever you did for one of the least of these brothers of mine, you did for me.

☆☆☆

Matthew 25:40 NIV

Perhaps you have lots of advantages. Some people don't. Perhaps you have the benefit of a loving family, a strong faith in God, and three good meals each day. Some people don't. Perhaps you were lucky enough to be born into a country where people are free. Some people weren't.

Jesus instructed us to care for those who can't care for themselves, wherever they may be. And, when we do something nice for someone in need, we have also done a good deed for our Savior. So today, look for someone who needs your help, and then do your best to help him or her. God is watching and waiting. The next move is yours.

When am I old enough to start giving? If you're old enough to understand these words, you're old enough to start giving to your church and to those who are less fortunate than you. If you're not sure about the best way to do it, ask your parents!

WOW
We are never more like God
than when we give.
Chuck Swindoll

Teaching generosity: It's never too early to emphasize the importance of giving. From the time that a child is old enough to drop a penny into the offering plate, we, as parents, should stress the obligation that we all have to share the blessings that God has shared with us.

Dear Lord,
You have given me so many
blessings. Make me a cheerful,
generous giver, Lord, as I share
the blessings that You first
shared with me.

Amen

18

It Starts in the Heart

Blessed are the pure of heart,
for they will see God.

☆☆☆

Matthew 5:8 NIV

Where does kindness start? It starts in our hearts and works its way out from there. Jesus taught us that a pure heart is a wonderful blessing. It's up to each of us to fill our hearts with love for God, love for Jesus, and love for all people. When we do, we are blessed.

Do you want to be the best person you can be? Then invite the love of Christ into your heart and share His love with your family and friends. And remember that lasting love always comes from a pure heart . . . like yours!

Pray early and often: One way to make sure that your heart is in tune with God is to pray often. The more you talk to God, the more He will talk to you.

WOW
Have your heart right with Christ,
and he will visit you often.

C. H. Spurgeon

Make Christ the cornerstone: Every family is built upon something; let the foundation of your family be the love of God and the salvation of Christ.

Dear Lord,
give me a heart that is pure.
Let me live by Your Word and
trust in Your Son today
and forever.

Amen

19

The Things
We Say

A good person's words
will help many others.

☆☆☆

Proverbs 10:21 ICB

The words that we speak are very important because of how they effect other people. The things that we say can either *help* people or *hurt* them. We can either make people feel better, or we can hurt their feelings.

The Bible reminds us that words are powerful things; we must use them carefully. Let's use our words to help our families and friends. When we do, we make *their* lives better *and* our own.

Think first, speak second: If you want to keep from hurting other people's feelings, don't open your mouth until you've turned on your brain.

WOW
Careless words stab like a sword.
But wise words bring healing.
Proverbs 12:18 ICB

Parents set the verbal tone: As parents, it's up to us to establish the general tone of the conversations that occur in our homes. Let's make certain that the tone we set is worthy of the One we worship.

Dear Lord,
make my words pleasing to You.
Let the words that I say and the
things that I do help others to
feel better about themselves
and to know more about You.

Amen

20

When People Are Not Nice

If someone does wrong to you, do not pay him back by doing wrong to him.

☆☆☆

Romans 12:17 ICB

Sometimes people aren't nice, and that's when we feel like striking back in anger. But the Bible tells us not to do it. As Christians, we should not repay one bad deed with another bad deed. Instead, we should forgive the other person as quickly as we can.

Are you angry at someone? If so, then it's time to forgive him or her. Jesus does not intend that your heart be troubled by anger. Your heart should instead be filled with love, just as Jesus' heart was . . . and is!

Forgive . . . and keep forgiving! Sometimes, you may forgive someone once and then, at a later time, become angry at the very same person again. If so, you must forgive that person again and again . . . until it sticks!

WOW
Forgiveness is God's command.
Martin Luther

A model of forgiveness: If you want your children to learn the art of forgiveness, then you must master that art yourself. If you're able to forgive those who have hurt you and, by doing so, move on with your life, your kids will learn firsthand that forgiveness is God's way.

Dear Lord,
make me a forgiving person.
Help me to forget past
disappointments and to forgive
those who have disappointed me.
Fill my heart not with bitterness,
but with love for others . . .
and for You.

Amen

Pray About It!

Do not worry about anything. But pray and
ask God for everything you need.

☆☆☆

Philippians 4:6 ICB

If you are upset, pray about it. If there is a person you don't like, pray for a forgiving heart. If there is something you're worried about, ask God to comfort you. And as you pray more, you'll discover that God is always near and that He's always ready to hear from you. So don't worry about things; pray about them. God is waiting . . . and listening!

Open-eyed prayers: When you are praying, your eyes don't *always* have to be closed. Of course it's good to close your eyes and bow your head, but you can also offer a quick prayer to God with your eyes open. That means that you can pray anytime you want.

WOW
If my heart is right with God,
every human being is my neighbor.
Oswald Chambers

Make your house a house of prayer: Prayer changes things *and* it changes families. Make certain that it changes *yours*.

99

Dear Lord,
You are always near;
let me talk with You often.
Let me use prayer to find Your
answers for my life today and
every day that I live.

Amen

22

When I'm Angry

A foolish person loses his temper.
But a wise person controls his anger.

☆☆☆

Proverbs 29:11 ICB

Temper tantrums are *so* silly. And so is pouting. So, of course, is whining. When we lose our tempers, we say things that we shouldn't say, and we do things that we shouldn't do. Too bad!

The Bible tells us that it is foolish to become angry and that it is wise to remain calm. That's why we should learn to control our tempers *before* our tempers control us.

No more temper tantrums! If you think you're about to throw a tantrum, slow down, catch your breath, and walk away if you must. It's better to walk away than it is to strike out in anger.

WOW

A person who quickly gets angry causes trouble. But a person who controls his temper stops a quarrel.

Proverbs 15:18 ICB

Parents get angry, too: as bad as children's temper tantrums can be, they pale in comparison to the adult versions. If you expect your children to control their tempers—and you should—then you, as the adult in the family, must also control yours. Otherwise, you children will ignore what you say and do what you do.

103

PRAY TiME

Dear Lord,
I can be *so* impatient, and I can
become *so* angry. Calm me down,
Lord, and make me a patient,
forgiving Christian. Just as You
have forgiven me, let me forgive
others so that I can follow
the example of Your Son.

Amen

23

Honesty is the Best Policy

Good people will be guided by honesty.

☆☆☆

Proverbs 11:3 ICB

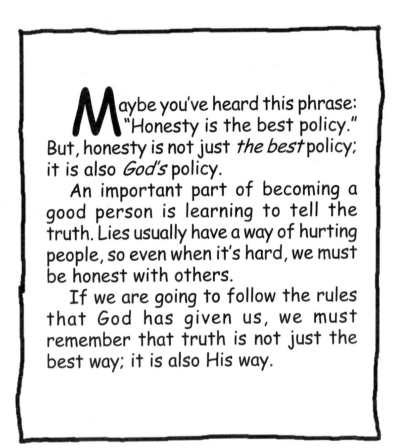

Maybe you've heard this phrase: "Honesty is the best policy." But, honesty is not just *the best* policy; it is also *God's* policy.

An important part of becoming a good person is learning to tell the truth. Lies usually have a way of hurting people, so even when it's hard, we must be honest with others.

If we are going to follow the rules that God has given us, we must remember that truth is not just the best way; it is also His way.

When it's hard to tell the truth: When telling the truth is hard, that probably means that you're afraid of what others might think or do when you're truthful. Remember that it is usually better to face those kinds of problems *now* rather than *later!*

WOW

The honest person will live safely, but the one who is dishonest will be caught.

Proverbs 10:9 ICB

White lies? Beware! Sometimes, we're tempted to "shade" the truth. Unfortunately, little white lies have a tendency to turn black . . . and they grow. As the prime role models for our children, our best strategy is to avoid untruths of all sizes and colors.

PRAY TIME

Dear Lord,
sometimes it's hard to tell
the truth. But even when telling
the truth is difficult, let me
follow Your commandment.
Honesty isn't just *the best*
policy, Lord; it's *Your* policy,
and I will obey You by making it
my policy, too.

Amen

24

What James Said

This royal law is found in the Scriptures:
"Love your neighbor as yourself." If you
obey this law, then you are doing right.

☆☆☆

James 2:8 ICB

James was the brother of Jesus and a leader of the early Christian church. In a letter that is now a part of the New Testament, James reminded his friends of a "royal law." That law is the Golden Rule.

When we treat others in the same way that we wish to be treated, we are doing the right thing. James knew it and so, of course, did his brother Jesus. Now *we* should learn the same lesson: it's nice to be nice; it's good to be good; and it's *great* to be kind.

Kind is as kind does: In order to be a kind person, you must do kind things. Thinking about them isn't enough. So get busy! Your family and friends need all the kindness they can get!

WOW

Let us not be content to wait and see
what will happen; let's be determined
to make the right things happen.

Peter Marshall

Kind is as kind does, Part 2: Your children will learn how to treat others by watching you (not by listening to you!). Acts of kindness speak louder than words.

111

Dear Lord,
it's easy to be kind to some
people and difficult to be kind
to others. Let me be kind to *all*
people so that I might follow
in the footsteps of Your Son.

Amen

25

Making Others Feel Better!

Let us think about each other and
help each other to show love and
do good deeds.

☆☆☆

Hebrews 10:24 ICB

When other people are sad, what can we do? We can do our best to cheer them up by showing kindness and love.

The Bible tells us that we must care for each other, and when everybody is happy, that's an easy thing to do. But, when people are sad, for whatever reason, it's up to us to speak a kind word or to offer a helping hand.

Do you know someone who is discouraged or sad? If so, perhaps it's time to take matters into your own hands. Think of something you can do to cheer that person up . . . and then do it! You'll make two people happy.

Cheering someone up without saying a word:
If you want to cheer someone up but can't
think of something to say or do, try drawing
a picture or writing a note.

WOW

If our hearts have been attuned
to God through an abiding faith in Christ,
the result will be joyous optimism and
good cheer which we then can
share with others.

Billy Graham

**Make time for "family cheering up" cara-
vans**: Do you know someone who is homebound
or hospitalized? Take the kids along for a
brief visit. Your children will learn that the
Golden Rule requires us to reach out to those
who need our encouragement and our love.

Dear Lord,
make me a loving, encouraging
Christian. And, let my love for
Christ be reflected through the
kindness that I show to those
who need the healing touch of
the Master's hand.

Amen

26

Let's Share!

God loves a cheerful giver.

☆☆☆

2 Corinthians 9:7 NIV

How many times have you heard someone say, "Don't touch that; it's mine!" If you're like most of us, you've heard those words many times and you may have even said them yourself.

The Bible tells us that it's better for us to share things than it is to keep them all to ourselves. And the Bible also tells us that when we share, it's best to do so cheerfully. So today and every day, let's share. It's the best way because it's God's way.

Too many toys? Give them away! Are you one of those lucky kids who has more toys than you can play with? If so, remember that not everyone is so lucky. Ask your parents to help you give some of your toys to children who need them more than you do.

WOW
It is the duty of every Christian to be Christ to his neighbor.
Martin Luther

Toy referees of the world, unite: It's almost Biblical: when two or more small children are gathered together, they are bound to fuss over toys. Use these disagreements as opportunities to preach the gospel of sharing (even if your sermon falls upon inattentive little ears!).

Dear Lord,
You have given me so much.
Let me share my gifts with
others, and let me be a joyful
and generous Christian, today
and every day.

Amen

27

Let's Be Cheerful!

A happy heart makes life a continual feast.

☆☆☆

Proverbs 15:15 ICB

What is a continual feast? It's a little bit like a non-stop birthday party: fun, fun, and more fun! The Bible tells us that a cheerful heart can make life like a continual feast, and that's something worth working for.

Where does cheerfulness begin? It begins inside each of us; it begins in the heart. So today and every day, let's be thankful to God for His blessings, and let's show our thanks by sharing good cheer wherever we go. This old world needs all the cheering up it can get . . . and so do we!

KiD TiP

Count your blessings . . . if you can! If you need a little cheering up, start counting your blessings. In truth, you really have too many blessings to count, but it never hurts to try.

WOW

A child of God should be a visible example of happiness, gratitude, and cheerfulness.

C. H. Spurgeon

Parent Tip

A house filled with laughter and love: Do you want to make your home life a continual feast? Learn to laugh and love, but not necessarily in that order.

Dear Lord,
make me a cheerful Christian.
Today, let me celebrate my
blessings and my life; let me
be quick to smile and slow
to become angry. And, let Your
love shine in me and through me.

Amen

28

It Isn't Very Hard . . . To Say a Kind Word

The right word spoken at the right time is as beautiful as gold apples in a silver bowl.

☆☆☆

Proverbs 25:11 ICB

How hard is it to speak with kind words? Not very! Yet sometimes we're so busy that we forget to say the very things that might make other people feel better.

We should always try to say nice things to our families and friends. And when we feel like saying something that's not so nice, perhaps we should stop and think before we say it. Kind words help; cruel words hurt. It's as simple as that. And, when we say the right thing at the right time, we give a gift that can change someone's day *or* someone's life.

If you don't know what to say . . . don't say anything. Sometimes, a hug works better than a whole mouthful of words.

WOW

We can properly comfort others
only with the comfort we ourselves
have been given by God.
Vance Havner

Coaching kids on what to say (and what *not* to say): We live in a world where common courtesy is all too uncommon. That's why it's important to teach our children about the importance of courtesy and tact. Does this sound old-fashioned? It's not! It's simply responsible parenting.

Dear Lord,
help me to say the right thing
at the right time. Let me choose
my words carefully so that
I can help other people and
glorify You.

Amen

Be Gentle . . .

Pleasant words are like a honeycomb.
They make a person happy and healthy.
☆☆☆
Proverbs 16:24 ICB

The Bible says that using gentle words is helpful and that cruel words is not. But sometimes, especially when we're frustrated or angry, our words and our actions may not be so gentle. Sometimes, we may say things or do things that are unkind or hurtful to others. When we do, we're wrong.

So the next time you're tempted to strike out in anger, don't. And if you want to help your family and friends, remember that gentle words are better than harsh words and good deeds are better than the other kind. Always!

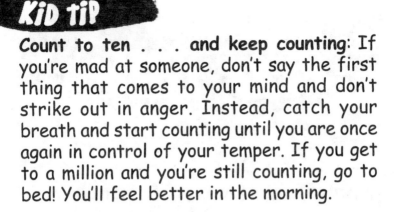

KiD TiP

Count to ten . . . and keep counting: If you're mad at someone, don't say the first thing that comes to your mind and don't strike out in anger. Instead, catch your breath and start counting until you are once again in control of your temper. If you get to a million and you're still counting, go to bed! You'll feel better in the morning.

WOW

I choose gentleness. Nothing is won
by force. I choose to be gentle.
If I raise my voice, may it be only
in praise. If I clench my fist, may it be
only in prayer. If I make a demand,
may it be only of myself.

Max Lucado

Parent TiP

Rest, rest, rest . . . Oftentimes, our anger is nothing more than exhaustion in disguise. When in doubt, get eight hours sleep.

131

Dear Lord,
when I am tempted to strike out
in anger, give me a forgiving
heart and a gentle spirit. Make
me a forgiving, loving, caring
Christian . . . today and
every day of my life.

Amen

30 Telling Tales

A person who gossips ruins friendships.

☆☆☆

Proverbs 16:28 ICB

Do you know what gossip is? It's when we say bad things about people who are not around. When we gossip, we hurt others and we hurt ourselves. That's why the Bible tells us that gossip is wrong.

Sometimes, it's tempting to say bad things about people, and when we do, it makes us feel important . . . for a while. But, after a while, the bad things that we say come back to hurt us, and, of course, they hurt other people, too.

So if you want to be a kind person and a good friend, don't gossip . . . and don't listen to people who do.

Watch what you say: Don't say something behind someone's back that you wouldn't say to that person directly.

WOW

The things you say in the dark will be told in the light. The things you have whispered in an inner room will be shouted from the top of the house.

Luke 12:3 ICB

Make your home a gossip-free zone: Gossip is a learned behavior. Make sure that your kids don't learn it from you!

Dear Lord,
I know that I have influence
on many people . . . make me
an influence for good. And let
the words that I speak today
be worthy of the One
who has saved me forever.

Amen

31

Kindness Starts with You!

We must not become tired of doing good.
We will receive our harvest of eternal life
at the right time. We must not give up!

☆☆☆

Galatians 6:9 ICB

If you're waiting for other people to be nice to you *before* you're nice to them, you've got it backwards. Kindness starts with you! You see, you can never control what other people will say or do, but you *can* control your own behavior.

The Bible tells us that we should never stop doing good deeds as long as we live. Kindness is God's way, and it should be our way, too.

Kid Tip

Kindness every day: Kindness should be part of our lives every day, not just on the days when we feel good. Don't try to be kind *some of the time*, and don't try to be kind to *some of the people* you know. Instead, try to be kind *all of the time*, and try to be kind to *all of the people* you know. Remember, the Golden Rule starts with you!

WOW

Hold on to what is good. Love each other like brothers and sisters.

Romans 12:9-10 ICB

Parent Tip

Mirror, mirror, on the wall: When you look into the mirror, you're gazing at the person who is the primary role model for your child. It's a big responsibility, but you—and God— are up to it!

139

Dear Lord,
help me to remember that it is
always my job to treat others
with kindness and respect. Make
the Golden Rule *my* rule and
make Your Word *my* guidebook
for the way I treat other people.

Amen

Bible Verses to Memorize

Do to others as you would
have them do to you.

☆☆☆

Luke 6:31 NIV

Be kind to one another,
tender-hearted,
forgiving each other,
just as God in Christ
also has forgiven you.

☆☆☆

Ephesians 4:32 NASB

A gentle answer turns
away wrath, but
a harsh word stirs up anger.

☆☆☆
Proverbs 15:1 NIV

Be gentle unto all men, apt to teach, patient.

☆☆☆

2 Timothy 2:24 KJV

Anything is possible
if you have faith.

☆☆☆

Mark 9:23 TLB

Blessed are they
that put their trust in him.

☆☆☆

Psalm 2:12 KJV

Be merciful,
just as your Father
is merciful.

☆☆☆

Luke 6:36 NASB

A new commandment I give
to you, that you love one another,
even as I have loved you,
that you also love one another.

☆☆☆

John 13:34 NASB

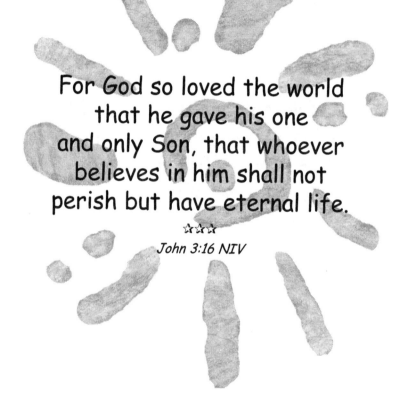

For God so loved the world
that he gave his one
and only Son, that whoever
believes in him shall not
perish but have eternal life.

☆☆☆

John 3:16 NIV

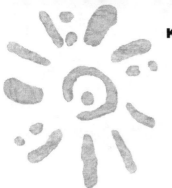

We love him,
because he first loved us.

☆☆☆

1 John 4:19 KJV

Don't be selfish . . . .
Be humble, thinking
of others as better
than yourself.

☆☆☆

Philippians 2:3 TLB

Freely you have received, freely give.

☆☆☆

Matthew 10:8 NIV

The LORD is righteous
in all His ways
And kind in all His deeds.

☆☆☆

Psalm 145:17 NASB

See that no one pays back
evil for evil, but always try
to do good to each other
and to everyone else.

✩✩✩

1 Thessalonians 5:15 TLB

155

In everything set them
an example by doing
what is good.

☆☆☆

Titus 2:7 NIV

Kindness

This is the day
the LORD has made;
let us rejoice and be glad in it.

☆☆☆

Psalm 118:24 NIV

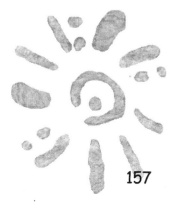